Kinetic Realms
—— *of* ——
Love and Beautiful
Poetry

Kevin R. L. Butler

Tulsa, Oklahoma

KINETIC REALMS OF LOVE AND BEAUTIFUL POETRY
© 2006 by Kevin R. L. Butler

Published by Insight Publishing Group
8801 S. Yale, Suite 410
Tulsa, OK 74137
918-493-1718

ISBN 1-932503-57-9
Library of Congress catalog card number: 2005924111

Printed in the United States of America

All Glory to God!
He is the Beginning!

Contents

To the Family of John Earl McCoy
Heavenly Hill (In sincere memory of LaVelma Hill)
Years
Forever
A Hundred Fold
I Do Know
Ms J.
Dear Lanette
We Thank You
Lust Not!
Happy Birthday Lanette
My wife or what ?
Classic Sports
Wanna Box
Spiritual Training
Ali
Hockey
Baseball
Brother-In-Law
Tennis
Michael Jordan (M.J.)
Protect Us
Football
Down Time Injury
You Don't Know Me!
Lawyers
Be Blessed
Is There Something Wrong (To My Wife)
goddess
My Wifey
It's Not Over
Thank You
Tiffany's First Bible

Acknowledgments

All Glory to God!

Introduction

A sample of poems with the whole world in mind
Feelings from the heart in these you will find

Just a few I have decided to share with you
Some of my life but all are true

So many different emotions that we express
in our time
So many different ways we choose to
release our minds!

The poems I have given are for all to see
There will be more in the future of K.R.L.B.!

So I dedicate this first volume to my earthly father
whom I loved
For his guidance had to be sent from the glory
that's above

For I know he was guided with God's Hands
For you can see from the poem on the next page, he
was One Great Man!

One Great Man

There are many great men that have been in this world
There's been many in the past and of some we
haven't heard
There are many in the Bible that we know much about
But there will be many in the future in this I have
no doubt
What makes a great man-it depends on your belief
He not only provides for his family, but he provides
something more deep
He teaches you to be grounded and have balance in
your life
You can have both of these with God to help you to
do what's right!
He must have the heart of a lion and decisions that
stand bold
For what he believes in he will stand up for until
he's a thousand years old!
Now I only know one great man that's been in my life
Because he stands for all of this and he's helped me
through my strife!
Yet there were times when we did not get along
God forgot to tell me this man could never be wrong!
Melvin L. Butler is that man that I loved very much
My soul belongs to God and in Him I surely trust!
Now great men have greater men that their wisdom
comes from

Their knowledge and their wit we must applaud some
I heard there's one greater man that taught my
great man-I may never be the same
And because of him I am a greater man and *Robert
Butler* was his name!

Part I

Poems of Love and One that is not!

True Love

I'm looking for my sister and she's no where to be
found
They say she lives on Belmont-that's not her, that's
some other clown!

Here's to my big sister who was never hard to find
Back then she was very big to me and also very kind

She taught me to take care of myself and to have fun
And to stand up for myself until my life is done!

The strength that she gave me only could have come
from her
Although there was one more power that made us all
say Sir!

I'm looking for my sister and she used to tell me she
loved me everyday
I'm looking for her guidance because she always
knows the way

So if you see my sister tell her I miss her very much
There's only one answer to any question *is* in God we
must only trust!

And tell her that I love her and I'll be here when she
gets back
Yes! Tell her that I love her-that's no brag, it's just a
fact!

Serenity

To a brother that I love-but I have something to say
You are mad at God because our father is not with us
today
Our father made his own decisions when we were
young
And the time we spent in those days was not very fun
He would have changed a long time ago but in alcohol
he did trust
Believe me he tried-but the devil's job is to destroy us!
Then he made a complete turn for God had something
to say,
"I love you very much and you will not go out this way!
For I know the time that has been wasted and I know
the pain your family has tasted
It's time for you to make peace before you come
home to me
It's time to show your children how loving you can be."
So God gave him more time to show us that he cared
Your fishing trips together you just can't find
anywhere!
My boys are two miracles from God, so we and our
father will never part!
So you still say brother he had turned his life around
God should have given him more time because our
relationship was found!
God is not a man to try to figure out what's in His
plans
For He holds not power but *all* power and time in His
hands
He is letting us know every decision we make will be a
seed
All seeds grow or die; from our father's life we must
take heed!

Blessed

To a young lady that I don't know very well
But you are surely blessed this I can tell
For when I see you-there's a glow for all
people to know
That Jesus is following you wherever you may go
It's not just your beauty, but there's something inside
That let's people know that is where God resides
So may your blessing continue and may all your
visions come true
And may you never forget how much Jesus loves you!

Passion

To caress the one that you care for and never hesitate
To hold that special hand that matches your
perfect taste
To shiver in your shoes with desire at
just a mere sight!
To intensively request one's presence
as if an appetite!
To have boundless greed that meets
the latest fashion
No, nothing can compare to true honest and
complete passion!

My Acknowledgement

My acknowledgement is of your beauty and I don't
mean to stare
The way you carry yourself is so appealing and I
also love your hair
So please except this poem of acknowledgement for
I really mean no harm
I'm just a gentleman that has acknowledged you so
there's no reason for alarm!
So may God bless you pretty lady and this kind
poem you have seen
And I know He will be with you and it's not
because you're a queen!

Hi!

There's a special person to whom I'd like to say Hi!
She's very dear to me and the apple of my eye
She has a heart that no one can touch
She loves me more than "just enough"
She misses me and I miss her the same
We can't be together because of a sick person's game!
But be patient my love we'll join hands once more
And nothing will come between us,
we'll maybe a door
I'm talking about that little person that I have to
look down to see
My very special little girl-*Miss Tiffany*!

Ex-Factor

Here's a poem just for you
To make all your dreams came true

You've become a thief and a coward, I'm sorry to say
They hung one and shot the other back in the day!

Both of these things won't happen to you
But one day you'll reap what you've sown and we'll
see what you will do

What you have done has been very bold
But wherever I live I'm still head of the household!

One more thing I forgot to say
These childish games you have begun to play

If you're not home by this evening you can keep
that key and that raggedy little house
Because I don't want to be married to a thief
nor a mouse!

Lady

To a very special lady I met recently
With a very special heart to which God holds a
special key

She has the class of a lady- and not like many I
have known
A good conversationalist when we conversed on the
phone

A heart of gold that not everyone knows
Compassion in her voice that could never be sold!

An understanding woman that all men should have
Whoever comes to her will never be lonely or sad

And a very sexy lady that possesses all the curves
Should be treated like a Queen, one to be served

So may God bless you pretty lady and all that you
possess
May you have all the love you desire because you
deserve nothing less!

I Almost Missed Out

I was out the other night guess what I saw
A beautiful lady that was across from me at the bar
I smiled at her and she smiled back
We caught eyes together and I thought that was that
As I begin to talk back to my friend you see
I felt as though she staring at me!
So I turned my head to see was it true
She was staring again and I knew what not to do
Something strange happened and I'll tell you what
Believe or not I started to blush
I stared back at her and that smile was there
One of the most beautiful smiles you'll see
anywhere!
So I backed away and you won't believe why
But in reality I'm really and truly a shy type of guy!
So I backed to the wall and thought I got away
Next thing I knew she was close and I didn't know
what to say
But her voice was so comfortable all the way to the end
I not only met a beautiful lady that night, but also
a beautiful friend!

First Contact

Okay you won! But it's not a contest that you can
win-I miss you first because you are my friend
A good friend is someone who talks the way we do-
about everything in the world & politics too!
I feel I can talk about anything with you-things
that are old and other things that are new
Good friends have good communication like us-we
had a lot in common especially our trust
Its okay for you to not feel the same-our friendship
you'll think of when you're in a lot of pain
I don't mind contacting you the way I did at first-
for a friend like me one day you will thirst!

House Full

When there's a third party that is in your home
You know something is wrong because you
are not alone!
When people go outside of their relationships
There is something at home they do not get
So whatever those things may be
Always be sure you can get it from me
But you have to talk to me and let me know
So I can fulfill your needs and we can grow!
And surely whatever I need I will not be afraid to ask
For I want our relationship to forever last!

Too Much Shelter

Here's a short story about a woman in love with a
beautiful pearl
She had more respect for it than anything in the
world
Her respect for it may have went too far
She would sit and admire it like a bright, shining star!
So much respect in hot weather it would sit under a fan
She wouldn't even wear it-not even for her special
man!
But the pearl did not take it as a thing of fame
The pearl took it as though she were playing a silly
game
One day she came home and the pearl was gone!
She knew not what she had done wrong
She thought she had given the pearl everything she
could detect
But what she had given the pearl was too much
respect!
Respect is something that should be given to
everyone
But too much of it like anything else spoils all the fun
Don't let it get between you and a friend you might
have
Or you may end up like the woman being lonely
and sad!
So you say my little pearl what does this have to do
with us?
I will explain it a little further if I truly must!
I've had the same type of respect for you-and I've
had it for a long time
That's why till this day you have not been mine!

The Last Days of Loneliness

As I sit here writing this poem
I wonder will I ever be alone
Although I've been with plenty of women in my life
It's been a struggle uphill as I searched for my true
wife!
I've been searching for a woman since I was very
young
Searching for the one to spend my life with till my
days are done!
Now I know my search was not in vain
Though the devil has tricked me causing a lot of
pain!
For he fooled me into believing in the method I
took
Which was to go to bed with each woman that had
a seductive look
But now I know through God's glory and grace
My wife has been chosen-He has set my pace!
And no longer will I have to chase
For what God has for me no one can give or take
away
If it's from God it will be mine and that's all I have
to say
Now I know that in loneliness I will never be
For He has promised to never leave nor forsake me!

Inflexible

There are things in my life that I don't understand-
things that happened that weren't in my plans
For I used to search out the things of this world
and they proved to keep my life in much turmoil!
The search for God's glory is now my destiny-in His
word and wisdom is where I choose to be!
For in His wisdom my answers will be revealed-
with Jesus' love and mercy I will be filled!
The visions I now hold of my future I clearly see
And He will bring them to pass because of the love
He has for me!

A Class Reunion

Here we are united twenty years later-a blast from the
past
The road we have taken to here-only God knows
how we would last!
There are some that are not present-who we have
lost through time
But their memories will carry on in us-in our
hearts and in our minds!
So let's take each moment of this reunion that we share
To spread love and kindness that you can't just
find anywhere!
May God bless us all in the future for we know not
what's in store
May He lead us and guide us through all of His
open doors!
And may He bless this poet who definitely will end
up in heaven
And may you all be with me, the Libbey High
School Class of "77"!

From Whence We Came

We came from a high school time where we thought of our life as in its prime!
Where the days were free and so was the rent and the money that we had was already spent!
The clothes we wore were in style and we succeeded to grow our hair as if we lived in the wild!
But there was love in our hearts that know one could really express
And I know this to be true-cause your here passing the test!
Then we left and entered another dimension, where happiness did lay but also a lot of tension!
So we made it to this point just as we'd planned-by now most of us realize that Jesus is the man!
What lies in our future-pray that our faith doesn't fail
But God knows what's going to happen-but us He won't tell!

Thanks for the Memories

We would like to thank the people that put this together
And the time that you spent in all types of weather!
Never any complaints, screams, or sobs
And we thank God for you-because you've done a great job!
But we all knew you could do this good from the start
And there's one thing you all proved-and that is to put something like this together as a group-One doesn't have to be very smart!

I Can See

Do you ever wake up and see the sunshine?
Do you ever look at a flower and say that's divine?
There are so many things to see
From so many different sides
Do you ever take time out to thank God for your eyes?

Where's God?

Where God's presence is I'll feel!
Where His happiness is I'll be!
Where His affection comforts I'll seek!
Where His peace lies I'll lay!
Where His love is I am!

Time

I was sitting at work and thinking about time
You know that element that controls your
life and mine!
Take your smile wherever you may go-its proof
that you will win
Every second is important so cherish them all to
the end!

Mercy Me

Nine lives that were spared by the Lord
Three days in darkness, without God's grace, it
could have been more
24 stories underground-waiting to die as the water
surrounds
No where to go and no one to hear your shouts
As the water ran faster and blocked every escape
route!
100 hours of battery power was their only light
Only 3 gallons of distilled water that God provided-
for He had them in His sight
The sound of drilling, He sent to comfort them in
this storm
Then the drilling stopped and again they would
start to mourn
Then my Father let them hear the drilling once
again, for He's not just our Savior but our friend!
Then a radio was lowered from above-in my eyes it
wasn't a radio but some of God's good love!
Is there a tragedy in this story-I don't see it in my
mind
It's a story of God's goodness, grace, and mercy-
that will last all time!
For in the darkness He might show up-even for
those that don't love Him a lot
It's His mercy and grace that will never stop!
For those covered by the blood of His son can claim
all victory for the battle has been won!
So when you think there is no light and darkness is
your only choice

Listen very closely; by the blood you'll hear God's
voice!
So you will never have to worry-it is a sin for you to
do
Cause He has promised to carry on His shoulders
all your burdens and your blues!
Our purpose here is for God to receive glory from
all gender
We were reminded of this-this past September-His
name will be praised-His mercy will be remem-
bered

Visions by Vianda

Welcome to the vision that God has made a reality
This is the beginning of what God has in store for
me!
For my visions are beyond these walls and they
will come to pass
For what God has in store for me-it will forever
last!
So sit back and enjoy the gift that I have received
God's given me this gift to make you beautiful, so
you will be well pleased!
And because He gets the glory, there's a blessing in
being here for you
For He'll keep you in peace while you're here and
even after I'm through!
So may God bless all that enter through these
doors
And may you live your life in excellence, in Him,
and in one accord!

Define

The definition of love does anyone really know?
We pray for someone to care for and also to hold.
We pray for understanding from the mate that we
may choose.
We pray to be treated fairly and not to be abused!
So if none of these you're getting and you still want
to be in love.
There's only one true love and it's from God that's
up above!

To the Family of John Earl McCoy
(In sincere memory of your beloved brother)

I'm here to tell you of some things that I know-
John Earl is in heaven, a place he's never been
before.
And you may ask me how do I know this to be
true?
He had accepted Jesus as His Savior and at that
time that was all he had to do!
I didn't know about his religious history-or the
things that he believed.
But I did know the kindness in his heart and all
the friends he did achieve!
As I sat by his bedside, through his eyes I saw his
heart.
He was ready for his heavenly Father to give him a
brand new start!
As he accepted Jesus to be his Savior, I saw the
love that was in his eyes.
I told him because you received Jesus, now you
can't and will never die!
He then gave me a look of comfort that could only
come from the Lord,
And that's when I knew for sure my Father had
opened His heavenly doors!
As I left the hospital there was no doubt in my
mind,
That John Earl was in heaven and by the blood of
Jesus he was going to be just fine!
So I must say to his loved ones and all the friends
that have loved him well,

He was saved by Jesus, for His love will always prevail!

And if you ever want to see him again-in heaven he will be,

But remember in order to see him-Jesus holds all the keys!

For it's by the blood of Jesus we are forgiven and by His stripes we are healed.

That's when your life will begin and God will say to your storm, *"Peace, be still."*

Heavenly Hill

As I stand here before you with sadness of the flesh,
God has answered my spirit-Ms. Hill is at perfect rest!
For He sent me to her to witness in His name,
And because of His glory, I saw for myself she
would never be the same!

As we glorified God together, praising Jesus as His son,
God placed on my heart, her life is not over-it has
only just begun!
As she accepted Jesus in her life as she may have
done before,
I saw for myself that God had given her His keys to
heaven's doors!

So may your tears flow with joy- for she now has
all insight,
For now she will live forever with God in His
eternal light!
For the light she now sees is brighter than her life,
For she will no longer see pain or darkness of night!

And her days from henceforth will never end,
For she will live forever in God's glory as His
heavenly friend!
And the love that she has shown will always remain,
And may it pour on your hearts as soft as gentle rain!

Years

I'm 5 years old and I love the Lord
Sometimes I need help to open really big doors!
I see things and people and I don't understand
But I'm willing to learn, I'll do the best I can
I need a grown up to help me out
I know there's a God, but I do have my doubts!
I heard that Jesus has the answer, He made all my toys
And I was told He could fill me with so much joy!
So will you teach me about Him-He lives in me
everyday?
Because wherever He's at-that's where I want to play!

I'm 10 years old now and I do understand
That Jesus is a King, but He was also a man!
But why did He make girls-my mom I know why
She already told me I was the apple of her eye
All other girls just get on my nerves
And they have weird names-who ever heard of a
girl named Pearl!
Enough about girls, I know Jesus is my friend
He died for me and you and all of our sins!
I'm 10 years old and I do understand
That Jesus loves me and likes to hold my hand
But why did He make boys, their not very clean-
they dirty all their toys-you know what I mean!
My dad is a boy but he really is a man and he loves
me more than any boy can!
Enough about boys-I know Jesus died on the cross
for you and me
He went to the devil and took some keys!

I'm 15 years old now and I think I know it all
I'm not really sure Jesus is there when I fall!
My parents don't understand-most of my friends
are not forever
I tell them there's a God-they tell me whatever!
But there is something inside of me-I want to do
what's right
When I know trouble is ahead of me-I fight it with
all of my might!
I know what I'm supposed to do-from my parents I
have heard
Speak to God everyday and diligently read His
word!
Then I will gain wisdom-and a leader I will be
Then all my friends in Jesus name will want to
follow me!
But this is not easy; peer pressure holds me back!
I need someone to pray for me because strength is
what I lack!

Forever

Now I lay me down to sleep, I pray the Lord my
soul to keep.
I *cannot* die before I wake, for I have eternal life
through Heaven's gate!

A Hundred Fold

There's a one hundred fold harvest that's going to
take place!
And because of the anointing of Jesus it will slap
me in my face!
And by His stripes I am healed and by His word-
the storm must be still!
Now this one hundred fold harvest is coming in
wealth-I'll pray for His wisdom -
I pray for His knowledge so I don't destroy myself!

I Do Know

I don't know what life's answers may be
I don't know if I hold all of the keys
I don't know why people do the things they do
I don't know if it's because of me or because of you!
There's one thing I do know as you read this poem
Jesus still stands tall on His Godly throne!

Ms J.

Here's to a woman that I know very well
She's not really my mother-but this you cannot tell!
A very strong woman that stands for what is right
A very loving woman you can tell that by sight!
So bless you Ms J. and not just for this hour-keep
trusting in God for He is your power!

Dear Lanette

I write this poem with friendship in mind,
Peace in your heart I pray it will find.
It has been sometime since I've written you a poem,
I would have sent it to your house-but you're not at
home!

I'll try not to be corny in the things that I must say,
But you know me, I can't help it-*I love you in all ways*!
Thanks for the ribs and the chicken you gave to me
yesterday,
The rest of the food I'll have to get some other way!

I only stopped by your house to make sure you
were all right,
Not hearing from you . . . too many days went by
and too many nights.
The confusion you have created has caused me
some pain,
But God has healing for you in His house in Jesus name!

It is more important that you know what *true love*
really is,
There's nothing you can do to me that I can't
forgive!
So as long as you will listen-God's word I will read.
As long as you hear my voice, I will be planting
God's seeds!

We thank you Father

We stand here before You Father by the blood of
Your Son
We thank You Father for the things You've already
done!
Then we thank you Father for the things you are
about to do!
We also thank you Father for our trust is in You
We then thank You Father for all mankind
And we pray to You Father Your love they will find!

Lust not!

I love you very much understand this you must,
But our friendship is more valuable than lust!
For sex is for a moment that will soon past away,
But the friendship that we share will last forever
and always!
We must put our focus on God and in Him we must
not part.
And then and only then-He will give us all the
desires of our heart!

Happy Birthday Lanette

Another birthday for you to be blessed,
For God has blessed you not like the rest!
For all may be blessed with what they see,
But only *you* my dear will forever be blessed with *me*!

My Wife or what?

I am not sorry for loving you the way I do!
I am not mad that you have not a clue.
I am not depressed that you won't marry me!
For it does not change my heart-you still hold the
key.
And this key that you're trying to throw away
might be picked up by someone else one day!
But the feeling I have will never be through, just
always know I am in love with you!

Classic Sports

A 24-hour sport channel-a dream come true
Watching sports from the past when there's
nothing else to do!
Reminiscing on old times whether good or bad
People in weird clothes that you use to wear to
keep up with the fads
But be careful with this channel it can be intoxi-
cating to all
Be moderate in all things that's one of God's laws!

Wanna Box?

A man in the ring biting and I don't understand why,
Supposed to be in the ring boxing, but instead
makes another man cry!

Tyson screams out "Allah," trying to send Holyfield
to the mat,
But when Holyfield screamed out "Jesus"-don't
think Tyson wanted to acknowledge that!

So I believe in one of those frustrating clinches,
Holyfield whispered Jesus in Tyson's ear and Tyson
didn't want Jesus' name mentioned!

So to his ear Tyson began to attack,
His unbelief in Jesus made him loose his mind just
like that!

Now Tyson's life is not over, he has plenty of money
to spend.
Best thing to do is to give up boxing, so his real life
can begin!

There are many directions he can choose from and
may he make the right choice.
May he learn from the past to get to his future by
listening to the right voice!

That voice is not mine, King's, Holyfield's, or no
one he can talk to on the phone.
I pray that he find Jesus, and then never will he
have to be alone!

Spiritual Training

Roy Jones is the best pound-for-pound boxer in the
world
This I have told you and this you have also heard!
It takes discipline and training to stay at the top
Day to day training with no ending or stop!
I'm in training right now, fighting Satan everyday
Throwing punches right and left showing Jesus is
the way!
My title won't be taken because of the faith I
depend on
And His word that I read will not die, but forever
live on!

Ali

The greatest boxer that has ever lived,
Boxed all around the world-and love he did give!
Only God could take a man who beat up another
And have him spread love worldwide like no other!
The shuffle-the jab-the greatest-he wrote it!
Confidence-compassion-desire-he sold it!
But he spread the love in Jesus name and he didn't
even know it!

Hockey

My mother was a good ice skater I am told.
So I said *"I'll try it once-but it seems to be cold!"*
So I went with my daughter for she said it would
be fun,
And it was until I was almost done.
I fell on the ice-I couldn't believe the pain!
But I got up and walked away thanking God in
Jesus name!

Baseball

I did play in the seventh and eighth grade.
My foot had gotten stuck under second base
because it rained that day
I heard this crack-I knew my ankle was gone
My coach came over and said "Get up there's
nothing wrong"
I looked at him like he had just lost his mind,
And I said with anger, "My ankle is not fine!"
I was in a cast for four months missed some of my
freshmen year of school;
Had a tutor come to my house-my friends thought
that was pretty cool!

Brother-In-Law

This is to my brother-in-law that I love very much.
You won't return my calls, so we can't keep in touch!
Keep in mind this weekend since you like Green
Bay,
I believe the Patriots will have something to say.
So keep in touch although it's cold;
And be sure to come over this weekend so we can
watch the Super Bowl!

Tennis

I heard your poem Lloyd and I listened well
The excuses you talk about you cannot sell!
And my game of tennis that you mentioned
Is beyond your universe and your dimensions!
So bring your racket and I'll take care of all solutions
For you to beat me is only in your mind, it's just an
illusion!
That serve you have will never pass me
It will be returned to you like I was Andre Agassi!

Michael Jordan (M.J.)

The greatest all around basketball player that has
ever been;
Not even he can remember all his wins.
May God bless you M.J. and all your kin!
And may you go with Jesus when he returns again!

Protect Us

Here we are Father to glorify your name!
By the blood of Jesus eternity we have claimed!
For Jesus bore our sins and suffered all our pain!
Now we ask for your protection as we play this game!

Football

Remember right now I am fifty years old,
My father said Jim Brown was the best to carry the load!
It's was hard to dispute this fact-because of the records he did hold,
And I do like the man-cause he refused to be sold!
But my favorite running back comes from the Bears,
And if I played football I would run like him-his name is Gale Sayers!
There's a madness in a man that he cannot explain.
During this time he seems to enjoy pain!
The pleasure of this pain only few men can resist,
He'd rather have it than your gentle, precious kiss!
You might lose your man and don't know the reason...
But realize it's nothing you've done-it's just football season!

Down Time Injury

A couple of months of down time that I have
But it could be much worse-It's not really that bad
It will give me time to put my mind at ease
My thoughts and my peace of mind will be my
siege!
God has surrounded me with nothing but love!
The kind that men fantasize about and angels
dream of!
Although I'm not like I was-which was quick as a
cat!
My training has not stopped-cause I'm not done I'll
be back!

You Don't Know Me!

For those of you that think you can copy my lines
You don't have my knowledge and you don't have
my rhymes!
So dig into your little brain and come up with you
own thoughts
If there's nothing there and it is empty it's not my
fault!
A safety slogan for an oil refinery
Your vision may be very keen-but you never know
what's behind that steam!

Lawyers

Mr. Vjay and Mr. Sweeney are two lawyers that I trust.
I need them at times for their knowledge is a must!
So I pray for them and the things they must say!
And by me praying for them, maybe less I will have to pay!

Be Blessed

You may have changed my life with the decision you have made
It makes it kind of tougher because I only have one leg
But don't worry about Kevin because he will be alright
God didn't leave me to come to you-He is also with me at night!
Of all the things that I will really need
It won't be no one else's pity for me!
But I thank you for time-and the lessons I've have learned
You will go down in my love history-a woman for whom I have yearned
And I thank you for my passion, which you have returned to me
It will come in handy in the future-in a place I cannot see!
I'm sorry about the past-and all the pain at your door

Please forgive me and look towards the future for
what God has in store!
Let's thank God together for the love we did share
It just wasn't meant for us to be a pair!
But what he has in store for both of us-a person
beyond our dreams
And with our patience and our faith in God-He will
show them to be seen!
And I'm sorry about the argument-for that was not
my purpose
I just needed your lack of love for me to rise
directly to the surface!
It was frustrating you not calling me and loving
someone I could not see!
God bless and keep you as He has promised from
above
And may your children grow up to be in Jesus-
which is surely God's love!

Is There Something Wrong? (To my Wife)

Is there something wrong with the time we spend?
Yes there is for it should never have to end!
Is there something wrong with the love we share?
Is it wrong because a love like this cannot be found
just anywhere?
Is there something wrong with the fun we have?
I can't see how because when I'm with you I am
never sad!
Is there something wrong with making love like we
do?
I can't imagine what because of the feelings I have
for you!
Is there something wrong with you showing your
feeling in return?
For you know I would never hurt you; and for you
only I will always yearn!
Is there something wrong? I can only answer it one
way-
Nothing's wrong with any of this for my love will
grow for you more each day!

goddess

There's a goddess in my dreams and I know she's
for real
I've seen her in the flesh-but her I cannot feel

Her curves swerve like the rivers of the Nile
Her skin as clear as precious ointment in a vile!

Her smile, like a horizon that's never been seen
before
Her freckles, her passion make you want more!

Her voice is that of an angel-you can see right
through
It's the innocence that's in her-she doesn't have to
lie to you!

Her dances are of a goddess and I know this to be
true
Her movement is hypnotizing-like a spell that has
bound you!

You know you have been chosen because there's
something she has found
It won't be anything you'll say because you don't
have to make a sound

In her presence there is beauty in this you will
have know doubt
Be careful in her essence you might just pass out!

My Wifey

Thank you for the time I had last night.
For I believe our love is true-our love is right.
We have some type of understanding that I've
never had before,
Let's look towards the future-who cares what's
behind those doors!

For those of the past are not important to me.
For God has made us new creatures for people to
see!
And the *Dates and Mates* class that we will take,
It will correct our love of many mistakes!

My love for you will continue to grow.
I will pray to God to love you even more!
There are blessings and cursing that will be our
choice.
Let us choose blessing with our actions and our
voice!

I know you work so hard, I told Jesus you said
"Hi!"
He said, "Get to church so you can pay your tithes!"

It's Not Over

Decisions are something you make beforehand
By actions alone you decide as a man!
And the things you decide might not be your will
If someone else in your relationship doesn't feel
what you feel!
But be not afraid to keep your head up
One day it will come again to fulfill your cup!
And when it does happen you'll feel it again
May Jesus be with you-Love never ends!
There are things in life that are not in your control
But time will pass and it all will be told!
So keep the faith and you will see
God has a plan for you and me!
For this pain is not something that will last
Trust in God and it to must past!

Thank You

To all who know that my father has passed
We all must leave-Only Jesus will last!
So keep your faith in God, and things will be
alright
I know he's with his father-sharing His light!
But we thank you for your love-and may your faith
be strong
Because in your faith you can handle this-and the
pain won't last very long!!

Tiffany's First Bible

Your very first Bible-you have received from your
Dad!
The one your Grandfather gave you-I'm keeping it
so don't be mad!
It's more important that you receive one from me,
As he showed me-it's my turn to plant God's seeds!
For you are to look in your future and not in your
past,
Keep these words in your spirit-for they will
forever last!
So remember God must come first only then will
you find peace.
He will move heaven towards you-and all hell has
to cease!
So with this Bible my love I do give
Only Jesus loves you more and by Him, forever,
you will live!

Brandy's First Bible

This Bible is for a special girl named Brandy
It's better than a lot of stuff-even candy!
For it contains words that God has spoken
And they will be true forever and that's no joken!
God gave Jesus His son so we could be free-He
loves us that much, yes, you and me!
Now we're more powerful than the devil-for God
has given us His might!
So the devil must step aside for he will lose the
fight!

So if you ever feel sad-God has given you a key
Just close your eyes-to feel better-and say, "Yes-
Jesus loves me!"
This comes from your friend K.R.L.B.

Our Family Tree

My mother, a woman of kindness and compassion-
for people she did care
At a young age I knew she was beautiful because
people would stop and stare
All the things she taught my sisters could never be
told
I wasn't very happy when they no longer had to
iron me and my brother's clothes
Her love will last in our hearts and not just for a
little while
I can still see her face as she laughs with her beau-
tiful smile!

This is for my sisters-They are special to me!
First is my oldest (Adetra) we call her Dee-Dee.
She's good with people-and she gets along with all.
God has blessed her to pick up people when they
fall!

Then there's Denise who has always been stable.
God has blessed her with patience-to bless people
when they're not able!
Her faults are few and not all can see,
Her biggest one is-she has trouble listening to me!

Last, but not least, it's Desiree!
She has the gift of gab and knows what to say.
When we were little sometimes my father wouldn't whip her!
She would meet him at the door-with his dinner and slippers!

Then there's my brother who name is Andre.
He never likes to lose that's true through today!
With electric football men he would give me a scare!
When I would beat him-he would throw them everywhere!
Back then I didn't understand, I just thank God my brother has grown to be a good man!

I have a cousin named Leah who is as pretty as a dove!
Her sister's name is Kirstie-she's just full of love!
They have a brother named Tony-he's left handed just like me!

Their mother's named Aerielle-who is a teaching sensation!
Her husband is Ben-the best basketball coach in the nation!

I have an aunt and an uncle that I miss very much!
They now live in Vegas, I should keep in touch.
Their hospitality is second to none,
When they had a get together everyone would come!

Bonnie and Theodis are their names.
And my love for them will never change.

And their two daughters I love to see;
Marylyn with all the education and all the degrees!
Teresa, my very special cousin right from the start.
She knows there's a special place for her-right in
my heart!
Daniel, David, Dwight, and Dale are her sons.
And all through our childhood we had nothing but
fun!

My aunts Diane and Athlene, who thought I was
cute!
They need to see me now-I look good in a suit!
Then there was my aunt Tina and her daughter
Kim, whose company was sunny.
And my aunt Gracie who always was funny!

And her daughters Pat, Tracy, and Stephanie, who
was cute as bunnies,
And her sons Dereck and Ed who always loved
money!

This was a sample of our family tree.
Oh! My uncle named Harold who was *always*
hungry!

Friends

I have a friend named Stretch and he's 6'9"
The tallest man that I know that thinks he's fine!
But it's the kindness he has within-
And I'm very proud to call him my very tall best
friend!

I have a friend named Money and his wife's name
is Tina-I've known them for a long time
Seems like forever they have been real good friends
of mine!
They are very true friends this I feel,
One thing we do is keep it for real!

I have a friend named (Melvin) Mabbit that all the
children just love!
For his kindness and compassion comes straight
from above.
His child-like manner helps him relate to all the
kids.
They don't even know how brilliant he really is!

I have a friend named Joe-we go way back.
Known him since kindergarten and that's a fact!
Our friendship is forever and will never stop
I knew him when we all use to call him Spot!

I have many more friends that I have not
mentioned
But because of their names I'll have your attention!
There's Big Dean, Geechy Dan, Rob Brown, and
Hang-man.

There's John-Boy, Tin Man, Rabbit, and Red
Robot, Ish-You-Don't and The Wood.
There's Boze, Bug, Tone-Oz, D-Brown, Spence, Sid,
Rob, Doug, Reg, Stone, Dollar Bill,
Flea, Good Cookie, Brother Gene, and Bell
A pastor named Chuck and a cousin named Dale-
and finally there's Bill, Pat, J.B. and Kevy-Kel,
Last, but not least is my friend Lloyd-he's the one
in tennis that I destroy!
And to all of my friends I have not named-always
remember I love you just the same!
P.S. Larry Gibbs and Mark Salter-more Air Force
buddies I haven't seen in 25 years
I pray to God He keeps you near

A Bathroom Break

God bless you as you stand here or sit on this seat
May you accomplish what you are doing and may
you be very neat!
Use the towels, if you wash hands, there's one on
the back of the door
And while God's blessing you of all things, don't
pee on the floor!

Should I Vote?

You are responsible for your vote,
You will answer to God if you don't!
Now how you vote is between God and you,
Pray, then vote the way He tells you to!
Not voting is a vote for whatever side the devils on-
if your vote is contrary to the word of God,
You help put the wrong people in office with your nod!
You're connected to them and their judgments will
enter your doors,
It's hooked to that devil you voted for!
If you'll vote in confidence and make your ballet a seed,
He will take care of you and all your needs!
Then the next four years no matter who's in power
or what that administration does,
You've been obedient to God-you'll be blessed from
above! (Thanks for the inspiration 'Red')

Part II

Poems from a Pastor's Voice

The Year of Compensation

This year will be different than any year you have seen
For God's glory will shine bold-if you know what I
mean!
His people will glow and you know who you are
You will get things returned to you from near and far!
Things that were taken that you didn't know you
possessed
Things from your ancestors cause they passed all of
the test!
And the businesses that you wanted will be waiting
for you
For you stood tall in His patience and you showed
love all through!
And these things that happen will be noticed by all
For your faith and commitment-God will show off!
So to all that will get a piece of Gods' glory
Get ready for a double portion-for you're not to
worry!
And for all who think this is not for you
Start praising Him now for He's working in you too!

First God

There's a spirit of Elijah that's upon the land
of boldness and courage that lives in every man!
God's people coming together having power like no
other
The enemy must flee-he must run for cover!
The transference of the anointing-you get to
partake from someone else
You must transfer it to others-it's not for you to
keep for yourself!
And anointing like an unbroken chain and this
earth it will never leave
Moving from one person to another and restoration
you will receive!
God will command the devil to bring back all your
stuff
Our supply is in Him and He is more than enough!
But it must be clear to you-God must come first
He will supply all your needs and never will you
thirst!
So it's the spirit of Elijah that lives in me so I will
never be the same
As I pass it on to the next generation-I can clearly
hear the abundance of rain!

The Battle

We are the teachers of this world
And many students will carry our sword
And we will help to reform this world
In the name of our Master Jesus; our Lord!

Your Decision

Cursing and blessing you must decide
Choose one or the other for you cannot hide!
If your faith is not in Jesus you are under the curse
And the peace that you look for your whole life you
will search!
For all of God's blessings are waiting for you
If He's the head of your life and in everything you
do!
For Jesus died on the cross for you and me
That our sins may be forgiven by God you see
And by His grace and mercy we are all set free!

Destiny

There's a place that you are going-that you will
receive double for your pain
Hitting the bottom, bouncing back and never being
the same!
It's not a setback; it's a comeback as you begin to soar
It's a place we've never been before!
And expect the Lord to be there and you have to
move from where you are
Pull up your tent and move to a new place that will
take you very far!
And go after it with all your might
For the presence of God will be in it and you may
not have to fight!
Spiritual steroids for flexing your muscles; means
nothing

When your tendons and ligament inside are doing
all the suffering!
It's time to keep God in front in everything you do
For He will take of the things that's been hard to
handle for you
And He has hid some things from you-riches
beyond compare
For when you are ready for them, He will pull
covers off from everywhere!
These covers will reveal wonders-things you
thought you couldn't have
But when God says it's your time, you can create
your own path!
Respect the men of God-with an anointing in His
name
There lies your security and covering-not to receive
it-you're the one to blame!
There is an intimidation that will be there-bringing
walls down with a certain shout
We will be stepping in as a family-and the devil in
Jesus name will be stepping out!

Sparrow's Nest (Homeless Shelter for Women)

For you young ladies at the Sparrow's Nest
Jesus is working for you and you're just there for a rest!
For in this storm you will not stay, but pass through
For Jesus has something better for you!
Stay in His word so your faith will grow
For He's working wonders in you this you should know
And for the volunteers that diligently help in His name
He has a blessing for you that is beyond all fame!

Are You Listening?

God's voice is louder than anything you can do
Your destiny is determined by what's inside of you!
Your faith must be built on a promise and a vision
For the source that it comes from makes it an easy
decision!
God's words that you have, have made you very smart
They will change your surroundings and come
aligned within your heart
There will be things and people who try to take it
away
Some fools can't be avoided, but you have no time
to play!
You will pray for these fools in Jesus name for
goodness sake
But it will be for them to choose whether or not to
bake in hell's lake!
For your faith is attracted to tomorrow's promise
that will last
And the vision you have in Jesus name will come to
pass!

Keep It!

The Lord is my shepherd and I shall not want
For if He does not supply it-I shall not stomp!
For I lack nothing because the Lord will provide
If He doesn't give me something, I don't need it-I
will still pay my tithes!
For He knows what I need and in time it shall be
With faith and patience, He will deliver it to me!

Welcome Holy Spirit

There's an anointing that lives inside of you
A spirit of excellence causes you to do the things
that you can't ordinarily do!

The Holy Spirit is a person with wisdom, knowledge,
and power
His job is to get results and then all things are
possible!

And the might that He carries will break yokes of
any kind
God getting all the glory is His purpose and that's
the bottom line!

A fresh start with prayer as you begin your day
Quick to repent-a ministry where there's fire in the
Holy Ghost way!

A sacrifice for God may be a place of exchange
Spend more time with Him and you'll never be the
same!

When the people and the things of this world
attack without warning
I'll let them and everything know I have the power
of the anointing!

So I won't be the defeated no matter what one
thinks or says
It's the anointing that lives in me that will show
me Jesus is the way!

We are Family

It's very important for us to gather and be family in
the church
Physically in the house-it is proof-for a home you don't
have to search!
Be careful of what you listen to and what your ears
will receive
There's a reason for connectedness that you might not
be deceived!

And know them which labor among you and are over
you in the Lord
Their job is to admonish you, give wisdom, under-
standing, counseling, and so much more!
For this leadership you must honor-show respect for
they're your protection
They keep everyone in the house flowing in God's
direction!

And there's a spiritual dimension-a level beyond one's
personality
A spiritual relationship that you have to close your
eyes to see!
Be at peace with everyone-exhorting them with their
best
To every man which is good they deserve nothing less!

Rejoice evermore-never ceasing to pray
In everything give thanks, feeding the Holy Spirit in
every way!
Despise not prophesying-prove all things that are good
Abstain from all appearance of evil and have patience
like you should!

Peace In

To get in the kingdom you must have righteousness and peace
When you show up in a place all anger must cease!
And those that decide not to receive it in His name
You will not loose yours-your peace will remain!
For peace is a part of the blessing-we can only be led to it by the Lord
There are times He will fight for you-He has another purpose for your sword!
But there are times you will fight for the right to sow your seed
You have fought for this ground for it's your harvest you will need!
Peace will show you when your harvest will begin
Take your weapons of war and use them to get your harvest my friend!
There's a lion in you that can show you're not a coward
But the lamb that you possess-the way of peace is the power!
The lion and lamb will lay down together one day
Pay close attention to the next thing that I have to say!
The way of peace is maturity-not thinking other people are less
For if you do-you might as well claim your self-righteousness!
You cannot move towards your future if you're tied to who you are at war with
The people you hate have control over you-and in God's kingdom you won't fit!
And when you are at peace one way that it will show
People will move towards you everywhere that you will go!

Take It Higher

There are different levels of influence you must
understand
Don't die in your level; qualify for the next level if
you can!

There are at least seven qualifying steps that you
will need
Study them carefully then take heed!

Responsibilities you will have-for no one else you
can blame
If you choose to stay at your level, if you choose to
stay the same!

And authority will play a role, understand rank
and position
For you must learn to receive orders-not of your
own decision!

And at the next level there will be stronger storms
But they will be on the outside-while Jesus keeps
you warm!

How you deal with your finances; and the keep the
next generation in mind
We will then see some evidence of that next level
you did climb!

It's Yours

God has given a dream-a vision of my future if you
know what I mean!
He's dealing with where I'm going-not where I've been
If He has given you a dream you have no choice but to
win!
A dream is worth waiting for-a little testing to see if it
will fit
But you have to see your harvest in order for you to get
it!
You must see that tomorrow will be better than
yesterday
And to see it in your visions and dreams is the only
way!
There will be people around you with hostility on their
mind
They cannot accept your dreams-because theirs they
cannot find!
A person will stop in their life-when they don't feel they
can go on
Shutting the door on their dreams-not understanding
they are wrong!
Cause once you get a dream inside of you-It can never
be taken away
For if God has put it there-It will be there to stay!
If you put it down it will always get back up-for if it's
from God you can't kill it
No one can destroy His stuff; so you are to squeeze on
whatever is inside you-
There is a reservoir you have not yet tapped
Then we will see what will become of your dreams-your
prosperity you have trapped!

In Peace

We can't allow the good things of God to be robbed
from us
Our situations and circumstances sometimes we can't
trust!
God will give us peace beyond our ability to under-
stand
He will make sure things are alright-as He holds us in
his hands!
Learn to be content in the state of life that you are in
Losing your peace-then you try to get it back with
something that doesn't blend!
Learn to be content when someone tries to make you
feel low
And be content when you have prospered-for you have
to let go of your ego!
People will come at you and try to hurt you with the
things they say
You can be at peace-you don't have to prove you
haven't always been saved!
Some people love money so much they will do a lot of
backstabbing
If you have to lose your peace to get it-it's not worth
having!
So keep your focus on God as your faith tells you why
and what you believe
And He will show you your future as you use forgive-
ness as a seed!
And you can't fix every body-some people don't want to
be fixed
Although you love them-but you can't lose your
peace-pray that they may get some of it!

Follow Me

Leadership is a process developed on the inside of
you
God looks at your heart-man looks at your outward
appearance this is very true!
The church is the bride of Christ people will be
attracted to
The bride is beautiful to look at so do all that you
can do!
There are sacrifices you must make-are you willing
to give up to achieve?
For something that is greater than you have now-
you must make room to receive!
Someone close to you may betray you-you must
know who's on your side
Thinking they were a saint now you know that
they aren't-no longer can they hide!
Breaking the power of misunderstanding having to
risk being misunderstood
Great leaders break that power and some people
understand like they should!
Say what you mean and mean what you say
If you didn't break the power of misunderstanding-
confusion and chaos is on the way!
There is a connecting point of every relationship
where one will receive and give info
Before your enemy can destroy you he has to
distract you-this is something you must know!
These disruptions are the evil in your life trying to
pull you from God's house
And the distracters will always slow you down
trying to steer you from your route!

And there are problematic people-the more you
help the more their problems grows
Some people are sent by the devil-so the door to
them you must show!
And direction you must be given accurately-
communicated to everyone in the same way
No room for alarmist and twister or we'll be misun-
derstood every day!
A leader will face persecution for he can manifest
power over nations
To stay in his leadership position he must not turn
to retaliation!
For the role that he will receive-cannot be estab-
lished over night
A test of time and seasons-a history of doing right
things right!

I'm Coming Out

When you hold someone or someone holds you down
The word oppression is commonly found!
People using words making other people feel low
Oppression possesses the soul!
A person will start to feel in his life he has been cheated
Worst thing to have is a spirit that has been defeated!
The power of the lie-the bondage that holds you in
You see yourself as helpless-no way you can win!
But if you ever get the truth-you can snap yourself free
God is seeing this oppression and he is not well pleased!
But you serve a God that knows how to turn it around
He's name is I am that I am and he's everywhere to be found!
God says He will be everything you need him to be
He says He will bring you out-but your not coming out empty
For He will restore you with who you are internally!
If you been truly bound up you would do anything for motivation
God says He will fix something in you to lift all your limitations!
And you take the wealth that has filled all the sacks
It will be too much for you to carry-so use your sons' and your daughters' backs!

Prophetic Journey

It's possible that you can be on a prophetic journey
and not know it
Searching for something you can't find-and can't
show it!
People find God looking for something that they
have lost
A prophetic journey causes you to recover some-
thing more than what you've tossed!
Trying to recover something you don't have-God
will use that as a set up
Bad things could be the best things that ever
happen to you -so get up!
The thing you've been looking for-causing it to shift
in your favor
Now God has your eyes on a kingdom-and that
thing you cannot waver!
Don't listen to the mountain-hear the Spirit-not
men
About this time tomorrow something great is going
to happen to you my friend!
Like a fire inside of you-God helps you even if
someone else hasn't
For the joy you share together-some may offer you
a straight jacket!
They don't understand what you've been through-
and this journey you have found
They don't understand how you love Jesus and He's
about to turn it all around!!

Prophetic Ministry

Prophetic knowledge belongs to the realm of the
spirit
You can see things before they happen and you
don't have to be near it-to hear it!
You can hear something in your heart-something
good is on the way
And no one can talk you out of it -no matter what
they do or say!

Prophetic ministry has an eye that sees internally
If you can't see it-you can't have it-you have given
your dreams away willfully!
It has a voice that speaks in line with what God
says
Dead dreams come back to life His way!
Speak God words-things that are not as though
they were!

Prophetic places sometimes are locked up in your
life-until your feet hit a certain place
For God will bless you at that point-for He has set
your pace!
And a certain person may unlock the things that
God has for you
Keep drama and trauma out of your life-stop
fooling around with fools!

When we are with other people-leave them more
than just good thoughts
Let them know that they are able-to receive the joy
Jesus has already brought!

Events and times and even songs will let you know
your very near
And acts that you do physically will release some-
thing spiritual that's clear!

Focus

It's time to press on toward our goal
To live up to the things that God has told!
Time to respond with the focus we must show
Then we will go farther and further than we've
ever been before!

Focus on Jesus and keep your joy through your
strife
What you look at the longest will become the
strongest in your life!
Broken focus will cause instability
And everything in you and around you will induce
insecurity!

A trail of your faith produces endurance
Your test may become your testimony-your mess
may become your insurance!
Focus on creating a great day-live one day at a
time
And learn to be content-in all ways be kind!

We've been called to be a blessing-It's our energy
we must pour
You will never run out-It comes from the presence
of the Lord!

It's going to require your finances-and that may be
where your focus is
You're only blessed when you become a blessing -
Then you will have much more to give!

When you feel weak into His presence you should be
He has your account in the spirit and only His
expectations shall be your seed!
Each of these poems deposits into my account
Every day He wakes me up-I'm already happy with
the amount!

A Process

Don't be pushed around by your problems
Jesus dying on the cross has already solved them!
Jesus has already dealt with your yesterday
From the power of all curses your spirit has been
saved!
Placement plays a role where your miracle will be
blessed
For all others to see-for them to be a witness!
Timing and opportunities windows and doors that
shall be opened
Seize this moment when they happen-seize the
time Jesus has spoken!
And your confirmation can't come from just
anyone's lips
It has to be confirmed by a higher authority-by
headship!
There's a principle of process-you will get cleansed
as you go
Little steps changing your world walk it out spiri-
tually as you grow!
The principal of the tithe the return of one out of ten
Everybody that starts out doesn't finish till the end!
You can have the biggest vision in the world that
over fills your cup
But if your body doesn't come-you won't show up!
The unexpected may happen-it's the law of the
underdog
No one gave it to you-so you fight for it all!

Move On

Teaching should come to you on a regular basis
Developing an appetite for the entire word of God
should be your taste!
People that don't have faith in God's multiplier
His creative power of choice works now to be set on
fire!

When coming to Jesus this is the moment, place,
and time
This is a good as place as any-to save God's people
that have fallen behind!
God's going to do it here and right now-it's ready to
come from him
A harvest is coming and we better be ready to take
care of all of them!

God always wants you moving by faith-a little bit
with Jesus
There is always enough and you don't have to wait!
Stop talking about what you don't have-and talk
about what you do
If God doesn't bless what you have-no one will
want it from you!

And if you give your life and time, seeds you will
sow
Jesus is more than enough and you will always
have an overflow!
So understand that this is the time for godly leader-
ship and our faith to rally
To energize and increase what's already working as
we take over God's valleys!

Time for Our Harvest

The Lord is beginning to draw people that should be
saved
Moonshine religion is a little bit of everything and
surely not the way!
Generations of people who are not being taught with
God's word
Some people have lost the taste for it-for the truth they
have not heard!

There's a distance between you and God because you
haven't accepted His commands
God made His people to know the truth-some preachers
just don't understand!
Jesus closed the gulf between God and man
A promise of signs, wonders, and miracles in your hand!

But they will mean nothing unless headship and struc-
ture is in your plans
To fellowship being a part of the church not just
attending it when you can!
We are here to make sure there is an act of worship
going up to the Lord
And a sense of stewardship, knowing together we can
do a whole lot more!

Atmosphere of praise ought to be in you when you get
there
It's not the ministry's job to pump you up-so don't just
sit there and stare!
So many gods-people haven't been taught right-
thinking the ministry will do all the work
But something should be on your life causing you to add
daily to the church!

May We Unite

Churches have grown not because of multiplication
but division
Not more saints-but more "aints" with confused deci-
sions!
Because its spiritual doesn't mean it can't be explained
God is a God of order and principles that never
change!

God will add his power to function by unity
When you shift the power of spiritual balance some-
thing big will happen in your community!
Enough people getting together and God being in the
midst
Expect something big to happen-as you are lead by
your headship!

It's a law-it's a principle-that means it's not about you-
blessings fall in unity
Jesus functioned by what His father told him to do!
The ministry's job is not to meet the people's needs
But to do as the Father says do-then we will succeed!

People are where they are because of what or who
they have joined with
When God has joined you together-you should not let
know one mess with it!
Join yourself with the right people so His order and
principle will apply
But if you don't make sure you are not the one he will
tell to step aside!

Another Level

There is an atmosphere for solutions-taking your-
self up is the only way
Your enemy can get stronger-if you opt to delay!
We have the power or option-the way our life must
commence
Increase is available by change-stagnation will help
in the resistance!
Resistance will be there to rob the desires of the new
A change is an indication your increase in God,
your next level is in front of you!
God will let you see your next level-then will pull
you back out
Did you learn anything or all you now have is
doubt?
Your level will be determined by the information
that you believe
Our beliefs are at different levels-in your faith you
must receive!
Change is what moves man from one place to
another
Your opinion and pride will stop you from going
any further!
We serve an unlimited God-an unlimited life we
should have
Your next level is from God-preparing you from
your past!
If it's of value, it has to be protected-that's the
reason for your resistance
The devil trying to keep you from that next level,
trying to keep it at a far distance!

The promise must be worth your investment-to use your time and all your plans
But you will have no choice to be rewarded-for God won't be in debt to no man!
We have come a long way on this journey under God's Son
God has promised to get us to the part of our life that's not yet done!
We wouldn't be here if it wasn't our time-the longer we delay-the more of a concern
That the enemy will have time to prepare for our return!
Do it when His grace is on you-for the final word He has
All things are possible in Him-Just read the story of Jabez!
The next level you're coming to-you will past the test
For with God being there for you-your latter will be greater than the rest!

The Atmosphere God Chooses

In the atmosphere God chooses, it's easier to be blessed
The movements of God are not equal it is a similar pattern of cause and effect!
There are churches, countries, and households where the curse may exist
And there is a reason why it is there-but you have to know how to access it!
We were created for his pleasure-but his pleasure is blessing us

A generous God we serve and in him we should only trust!

He has chosen to bless a certain atmosphere-Its one that you must create

Not with doubts, but faith and forgiveness must be your fate!

In an atmosphere of unity and agreement, He will dwell

Not division or strife, but a spirit of excellence-you must excel!

If He chooses to bless it-you must do your best

Not complainers, nor those who murmur, and certainly not those who disrespect!

He's God no matter what-don't deny him of his pleasures

He is moved by your praise-maybe then He will share His treasures!

We serve a generous God-He's looking for someone to bless

Follow His word and what He says and you'll be blessed above the rest!

He's a God of expectancy-with excitement on your mind

With your praise and your worship-says His word-its seed and harvest time!

He dwells in the atmosphere of generosity-with the stingy He will not stand

Not to share your time with Him or not to praise Him with your hands!

With the stingy He will not hang out with-saving your praise for something amiss

He's given you breath to breathe-but yet you show your selfishness!

You give to the house of the Lord-to be obedient to
what he has said
Not out of necessity but generosity-For by His word
you are fed!
But be a generous minded person and not just
because there is a need
Let generosity be your nature-for God will one
hundred fold harvest that seed!

The Power of God

We serve a God of power who is on a different plan
Not of politics, sports, or military-His power is not
the same!
An unlimited God by your faith He will move-He
has said in His word
"Is there anything to hard for me to do?"
He has the power to set all the captives free
Counseling is not a benefit, unless of His power you
have a key!
It is time for power ministry to return to the
church
For His power and His healing you should not have
to search!
The devil is real, no matter what they might say
He is working against you, *"It's not just another
bad day!"*
The power of the devil-only in Jesus name he will
flee
He's trying to devour you; he's not the Easter
bunny!
The power of God comes in like a flood

Breaking yolks, lifting burdens, leaving nothing
but love!
When you have been touched by His power you
don't have to understand
He can't be figured out or put in a box-He's the God
of all power and not just a man!
A God that will restore His people in one step, not
ten
He's not scared of your demons or the trouble
you've been in!
He's the power shifter in your life-He's the power to
be free
Filling the glass of your life-because it is empty!
He is the healing God-never has He made anyone
sick
He has made your body, so *He* can fix it!
Whether a headache or a tumor-in Jesus name you
can be healed
Resist the power of the devil and no pain you will
feel!
And when it doesn't happen the way you want it to
You lower your hands-for your praise is through!
And you say when I praise Him-it's extreme
He's there when I need Him on His shoulders
I will lean!
In blessing He will bless thee as His power is
released
A debt cancellation God-all your bills at His feet!
Favor coming in our direction and curses are being
reversed
Not because of what you've done-it's Him who loved
us first!

The power of God our salvation-going to church
doesn't make you saved
It is the power of God that will deliver you-it's the
blood of Jesus that has paid!
You can be saved from the penalty for it's time for
something to shift
Go to a service that makes the devil nervous with
your praise God's power won't quit!

Breaking the Glass Ceiling

We must break through the glass ceiling to get our
territory enlarged
To have a mentality of just enough will not take us
very far!
Something in that extra mile will get you that raise
You will excel above average-your recognition will
never fade!
The church represents the kingdom-crispy creams
won't do
People want to be a part of the kingdom-but it
must be a reflection of you!
A great God, a great praise, a God of love you must
reflect
Your will and his will should not be at odds-they
must in all areas connect!
Churches produce certain kinds of Christians-in
their culture it will show
Go somewhere you can become what you see-where
you want to be what they grow!
Forward thinking- ahead of the curve, no twenty
years behind

This is the information age with sharp ideas,
breakthrough Christians with innovative minds!
Manifestation without weirdness-clicking your
heels together must stop
Pouring milk on some churches, so weird, they go,
"snap, crackle, and pop"
There's enough power of God to press in-enough
miracles that will never end!
With the weirdness the community we can't win!
Punctuality is the virtue of princes-you are limited
if you are late
If you don't have authority over your alarm clock,
the devil will control your fate!
Take part in services active learning and listening
too
We go from watching to experiencing the message
because its part of our breakthrough!
A culture of experience that releases freedom to
expect people as they come
Not cookie-cutter Christians, but carrying each
other and then some!
A culture that embraces order that will help you all
of your days
Disorderly churches grow disorderly Christians not
following directions-your job can't be saved!
Increase comes with integrity, the sale of chicken
dinners must cease
Through our tithe and offering His principle says
we will increase!
Generosity-minded we are not here for just a
season
To be planted is one of our reasons!
For the next generation will stand

We're teaching them to possess the land!
Identifiable leadership-you're not a leader because
you want to be
If you are not appointed by the house you can't
serve coffee, tea, or prophecy!
Recognize your leaders after the service is done-you
don't hand your child to just anyone!
Ministering members do something for someone else
Volunteering your time-quit just thinking about
yourself!
We are Christians of the spirit of excellence that
has spoken
With God on our side-the glass ceiling will be
broken!

The God-Factor

You must embrace the word of God; then no longer
will you have to search
Receive the commandment of blessing, for it cannot
be reversed!

When you wake up to the fact God wants to bless you
A shifting takes place to do the things you couldn't do!

If you take God out of everything you may lose!
The three Hebrew boys should have never come
out-they should have been burnt up and abused!

If God decides to bless you-it's the blessing of God
you will get

He will reverse the curse, but not the blessing;
nobody can talk Him out of it!

Everyone's looking for an edge when their natural
ability is at its end
Spiritual powers that are off limits; contacting your
fortuneteller friends!

About the time you're ready to give up and your
hands are ready to drop down
God is not a man that he should lie; *Jehovah-
Shammah* will be around!

Remind yourself there is a God-Factor when you've
done all that you can do
Remember He's someone in your life nobody can
take from you!

There are some things you must study, then do in
the natural way
But when you come to the end of it nobody can
factor in what God may do or say!

You can't live without the God -Factor-it's trying to
bring you in
Everyone knows it is there and you should pray for
all of your friends!

People at the point in their lives where break-
through or breakdown is their only choice
Some things you can't do by yourself, so you listen
for God's voice!

To understand the God-Factor you have to believe
in the power to be blessed
It's not over if someone says *"no"* for it is God that
has said *"Yes!"*

You have to believe trouble will come and some-
times last more than just a day
A blessed man brings forth fruit in his season and
trouble doesn't last always!

Remember the power of the unexpected there is a
great person inside of you
Nothing will change on the outside until your
insides decide to move!

The first purpose of words are creative-*"Life and
death in the power of the tongue."*
What you say about your world you will live out till
your life is done!

There is a place God wants you planted to get the
God-Factor working
A place for you to be grounded, so He can take care
of all that is hurting!

And it's the power of the praise, the reason that
you are here
To tell Him how great He is, and then all hell has
to fear!

Get-Cha Praise On

Searching for your destiny in your praise it is
found
Worshipping Him with adoration and honor as you
voluntary bow down!

God and the devil have something in common, both
desire your praise
Only God deserves it, while the devil will send you
off to an eternal maze!

If the devil beats you at worship, calamity will be
at every turn
You will start looking to him for comfort then with
him in the lake of fire you will burn!

Prayer is very important of a selfish nature it can be,
As you ask God for the things you may or may not
need!

When you pray He may send somebody or some-
thing to answer you for your health
But when you worship and praise He has promised
to show up personally himself!

A lot of people cannot praise Him-for the pain of
their past
Praise Him in and out of season and it's your
future that will last!

The devil is the prince of power of the air

You control the environment with noise, it important
for you to care!

For the Holy Spirit rides on the waves of sound and the
devil does too
What kind of music that plays in your house, which
power will you choose?

Praise and worship is the answer to any trouble you
may have
As you praise God through it at the devil you can laugh!

But remember He doesn't need your praise-He's
omnipotent in power
It is you that need to praise Him-for He's the ever-
lasting tower!

The culture of this world should not dictate the courage
you have for God
Be obedient to Him and you will conquer all odds!

The preached word is from the written word, which God
puts before His name
But the living word is what shows up when you're in
the fire in pain!

The spirit of God will destroy people that like to control
what you do
With your obedience and worship He will also destroy
the demons that are inside of you!

At all times in your life, whether things go right or
wrong
Give God what He deserves, *"Get-cha praise on!"*

Just My Imagination

A piece to a puzzle I can never find
Does this piece really exist or only in my mind?

I started this puzzle some time ago
If I was going to finish it, I really didn't know!

For the pieces that I started with were on the table
in a mess
But it gave me a challenge at that time to past an
ego test

As I sorted out the pieces one would fall onto the
floor
I would go to pick that one up then I would see
many more!

As I returned to the table to my amazement what
would I see?
Some pieces put together there was someone
helping me!

But as I scanned the room and know one was there
I know I didn't do it so at least someone cared!

Picture this-I have the puzzle together and the last
piece I didn't see
Then looking under the table I said, *'That's the one
that holds the key'*

As I started to put this last piece in to finish this
puzzle kit

Know matter which way I turned it-It still wouldn't
fit!!

You're not going to believe this but I'll tell you
anyway
I've put this puzzle together many times and some-
thing different happens each day!

One time a piece was missing and I took it all
apart
When I put it back together that piece was there
from the start!

But then another piece was missing-I just couldn't
understand
Where were all the pieces going, this wasn't in my
plans!

Have you noticed I didn't mention what the picture
of the puzzle would have been?
It doesn't make a difference if you don't have God
in it, no puzzle will be complete my friend!

I was glad . . .

There is a house of the Lord where me and my
family attends
God's anointing is there and we are all His friends!

The leadership in this house is of God's love and
His power
We believe in our inheritance we lend and not borrow!

We believe that every word of the Bible is true
But it can only come alive with the power that's in you!

Our children's ministry is approved by the Lord
For it's the next generation that will carry His
sword!

We praise Him together raising our hands in song
An excellent place to get together and get your
praise on!

A place of healing and deliverance where miracles
begin
Where Jesus works on your heart to get rid of sin!

Where all are welcome coming in all types of
weather
Because God has said let the nation come together!

Every color of God's people coming from near and far
Our agenda is to worship the Lord so come as you are!

A place where freedom reigns where judging
doesn't come from us
It's the Holy Spirit's job to rid you of your lust!

So come join us in the house where you will never
be alone
It's a place of God's presence that's Toledo
Cornerstone!

Part III
A Couple of Holiday Poems

Happy Mother's Day
(to Lanette M. Butler)

You are a very good mother-this I have seen
You give all to your children-and your house is very
clean!
You cook when you don't have to for people that are
not there
I eat all the leftovers and I don't have to share!
And you work so hard-sometimes it makes me
upset
That I can't help take some of the load, so you can
get some rest!
But it's not me that can take the load off-deep
down this you know
Only Jesus can do it-it's your faith that must grow!
But I'm not here to preach, but to tell you what's
real
The love you show for you're children I wish all
children can feel!

Happy Mother's Day
(to LeaAnn Lusetich)

For a mother that I know that has done a good job
There are children in this world for your love they
would rob!
May your children recognize you for the love you show
And may they take your love wherever they may go!
God bless you pretty lady and for your future you will see
God has more love to give-for this is the key!

Happy Mother's Day
(to Barbie Clifton)

This is for a mother that is doing what's right
Loving and caring for her children with all of her
might!
The patience that you show can only come from above
It can only come from Him and it's called *Jesus-Love!*
But to show them how to love you must bring them to
God's house
To guide them and lead them in Him we have no
doubt!
For they won't be with you always and He will protect
them from all harm
In His protection there is love and no reason for
alarm!
So may this Mother's Day bring you all the joy that's
in your heart
And now that you are healed-from Jesus may you
never part!

Happy Mother's Day
(to my most Beautiful sister)

To a sister that I love more than time
You are a good mother just like mine!
The care you have for your children I see it is of love
And they will care for you one day as a bear does its'
cub!
So may this day bring you plenty of joy
And may God bless you with grown-up toys!

Happy Mother's Day
(to Bertha Riley)

To a mother that I have known all of my life
You have watched out for me both day and night!
The love you have showed only can come from a
mother
For I have slept on your couch and have woken up
with cover!
The love I have for you it will never be less
For you are very special to me more than all the
rest!
And although you don't see me very often-you are
in my prayers
For God bless and keep you for your love is so rare!
So may this day bring you happiness you have
never seen before
And may the love that you show open the hearts of
many more!

Much Love Mom
(to Sylvia L. Johnson)

To a very special lady that I love very much
I may not show up at your party, but I will stay in
touch!
For it's your motherly love that has planted a seed
And you're caring and kindness is all we need!
So may God bless you pretty lady and the things
that you say
For you will make a perfect angel in heaven one
day!

Thank You Jesus

Something about a birthday that gets more impor-
tant with time
I'm not only talking about yours, I'm also talking
about mine!
The key is to have them as they come and go
Because if you didn't, only God truly knows!
So thank God for those in the past and those that
are near
Thank Jesus for them all, especially the one that's
next year!

Happy 18th Birthday

This is for a player that has all the girls
But this birthday will bring you into a whole new
world!

For as time will past and you will see
Life has a lot more responsibilities!

But you will be alright if you trust in the Lord
For He will fight your battles for you with His
mighty sword!

But be careful my brother and pay attention to
where you go as well
For there are some so-called friends out there that
will take you with them to hell!

To My Friend's Wife on Her Birthday

Here's to a pretty woman I don't know very well
There's love in her heart this I can tell!
You ask how I know for this to be so
I see her love through her husband's glow!
Their love I know will endure until the end
He's not only her husband, but also her friend!
So may God bless you pretty lady and many more
birthdays you'll receive
He's brought you both together because you'll be
more powerful as a seed!

Happy Birthday

This is a poem for a special girl
On this special day in God's special world!
This day is special to me as I will explain
Every since I've met this girl my life has changed!
A beautiful girl was born on this day and I think
she likes me-*what more can I say!*
My vision's 20-20, I know it's not in my mind; she
might not think so, but the girl is real fine!
The feelings I feel-I'm not sure they are right
I've begun to think about her all day and all night
I trust my feelings in every way
All I want to do now is to wish her a *happy
birthday*!

We Wish You a Merry Christmas

What about the man in that big red suit?
You know the one that's fat, jolly, and wears those
black boots!
The children believe in Him-now that's really wild
Riding in a sleigh with reindeer-No Way!-No How!
There *is* someone spreading something at this time
of the year
And it's contagious to all because of its good cheer!
I got it! It's true! He's God's helper from above
But He's not here to spread toys, but to spread
God's love!

Happy New Year

So another year has past, so you to say to yourself.
Have I done the right things? Was I worth my
wealth?
Did I do more than just put a smile on my face?
Did I do anything to help my human race?
I think about the good things as well as the bad.
I think about what has made me happy and also
sad.
In this New Year I pray to listen and also hear,
With Him by my side, I have nothing to fear!
So I thank God for making it through and pray the
right things to do.
So God bless you all and Happy New Year too!

Part IV

Poems from an Answering Machine

Everything Must Praise Him

I'm watching the animal channel you see
And the animals are surviving just like you and
me!
They work for their food and shelter from the land
But there is one thing man still doesn't under-
stand!
The sounds they make are not friendship calls
Nor the emotions that they express of beauty that
says it all!
Their movement and praises come gloriously in
accord
Because He has said let everything that has breath
praise the Lord!

Think

Here's something that makes you think
If you feel that your life is about to sink!
There are a lot of people out there that have
nothing at all
But they know how to get up when they fall!
The power it comes from is not of this earth
Because the power here has Satan's curse!
It comes from the power that's up above
And you know that power is God, who is love!

I'll Be Back

Let's get back to basics if you know what I mean
I'm not available to talk or to be seen!
But if you leave your name and number-at the drop
of a hat
I'll be sure to get with you as soon as I get back!

Not Today

You cannot leave a message, which is beyond my control
There are people out there that I don't want in my world
So since you did try to contact me on the phone!
Leave your number on my pager and I'll call when
I get home!

You're Thoughts

Your subconscious does not argue with you
Whatever you think, it accepts to be true!
You have the power to choose health and happiness
Take these and use them-this I suggest!
But if evil is a part of your daily thoughts
You're stealing stock from the devil, but you won't
get caught!
So remember you're the captain of your soul and
the master of your fate
May you choose the right choices-may you choose
the right mate!
So may God bless the good thoughts of your
subconscious mind
Cause without Him your nothing-He's all love
that's divine!

How Important

If I don't answer this phone there are two reasons
at hand
Either I'm sleep from work or I'm looking for land!
So don't get discouraged leave a name and your
number
And when I return I'll call you back sure as God
made lightening and thunder!
But if that's not good enough you can page me with
pleasure
It's not the message, but it's our friendship that I
do treasure!

"...but of power, love, and a sound mind"

The definition of fear you should have down,
But I have something to add to it that will make it
profound!
Fear to do the things that you know are right,
Will keep you awake both day and night!
Fear to set aside all of your foolish beliefs,
Is something you have to pay for and you may also
have to weep!
Fear of acknowledging love that has been shown
There will be only one fear left and that's to be
alone!
So there's only one fear that I can understand,
That's the fear of God-and He loves me more than I
can!

That's Funny

Time to tone this message down for awhile
And talk about the things that really make you
smile!
They say exercise is what you need for good health
If there's no time for it-laughter takes its place in
wealth!
So try to put a smile on someone's face that anger
and hate you may erase!
Some will fight it until the end, they may refuse to
enjoy it, and they may refuse to bend!
But you'll be really surprised what laughter can
make you do
If nothing else, it keeps all the miserable people
away from you!

Power

There's power in one's voice that can make another
person listen
There's power in the law and we must abide by
their decisions!
There's power in violence that makes us do what's
wrong
But there's a price to pay that can put you away for
a time that is very long!
So take my advice and stand by the power that's up
above
Because out of all the power that's around-the
strongest is the power of God's love!

Express It Now

If you need a poem I'm the one
To fulfill your life with more than fun!
For every occasion that crosses your mind
For every emotion to cover all time!
So call this number for I need to talk to you
To write a poem to have your feelings come
through!
So if there's something in your heart that you want
someone to feel
Call me at this number and just be still!
When emotions fill your heart and you can't get
any rest!
Let me write a poem for you to erase it from your
chest!
Leave your name and your number and I'll give you
a call
I'll write a poem for you that can cover it all!

Madness

I have a story to tell if you think it's not true
Call me back later and I'll prove it to you!
Lies can be told in many different ways
Like a shrug of the shoulders or with nothing to say!
But the lies that you tell will make people sick
And God doesn't like liars-you may end up in hell's pit!
So if you don't want to meet a ghost keep the lies to yourself
And that's better for you and a friendship full of wealth!
There's a certain kind of feeling that's hard to explain
Can make a person feel inside like they've been played like a game!
It takes you to a place of emptiness that all cannot tell
There are a lot of sad feelings in the world and one is betrayal!
Let me share something with you that gets on my nerves
A person that lies has no place in my world!
So you can be as deceitful as you want and think my mind is in a slumber
But sooner or later I'll make you realize-you're dialing the wrong number!

He Knows

I don't know what life's answers may be
I don't' know if I have a key!
I don't know when my life will fold
I don't know what the future holds!
I don't know why people act the way they do
I don't know if it's because of me or because of you!
There's one think I do know as you listen on this phone
That Jesus still stands tall on His Godly throne!

I Care

There are people who care about you who you don't even know
And that caring stays with you wherever you may go!
They stay by your side and they're not even there
Because your joy and your pain they are willing to share!
So don't be afraid of this love that's condoned
It's wonderful to be loved so just pick up the phone!

Peace

Life is so busy, never enough time
To do all the things that you have on your mind!
In order to think clearly and keep your brain from a mess
The most important thing you need is God and good rest!

Seasons

Tis' the season to be right
Not to scream, fuss, or fight!

To treat each other with compassion and love
The way you are treated by Jesus above!

A special time for those who are dear,
But there's something more important I want ya'll
to hear!
You should have been doing this *all* through the
year!

It's time to change this message; it's starting to get
old
The New Year is here and let it be told!

There will be more smiles on my face than the year
before!
But let us not forget where these smiles come from,

They come from above
And I'm thankful if He just decides to leave me a
little one!

There is spring, summer, winter, and fall
Out of all these seasons there's one that stands tall
That's the season of love-for He covers them all!

Part V
Poems of Closure

In Front of You

This was the first volume of many to come
God's given me a gift and He's told me to
share some!

All glory to Him for I could not have done it
on my own
For He has given me the power to write all of
these poems!

And these poems you should listen to for this
I am told
He has given me a voice to express them in gold!

The way to hear the other gift He has given to me
You will be happy to know this book will be on CD!

So may God bless you and all you have learned
And may He bless the people that are in your
concern!

And I've saved the best for last
For the children in the future and also in the past!

For it's the next generation that will bring this
world back to the Lord
We must each teach them His word and they must
praise Him in one accord!

Children

Let's talk about the most important people in life
It is not your husband, nor is it your wife
It's not one of these you think it is
It's those bad little ones-God's wonderful kids!
You must be as a child to enter the kingdom of God
Then life will be heaven and no time to sob!
It's their forgiveness and innocence that's second to none
Then we know heaven's a place with nothing but fun!

A Child's Prayer

God is love-God is power
We thank Him for everything, for even an hour!
We know what's right-we know what's wrong
We pray to make the right choice to live very long!
We pray for understanding of things we don't know
We pray for His love and for it to show!
We thank You Lord for everything there is
We know Your power although we're just kids!

911
(Remember Then Turn)

Behind us are the days, which come from our past
Connection to the future in whose strength will we last!
The misery of evil is alive and well
But it will birth God's goodness-for His love will prevail!

We have been shocked, angered, and no peace we have
found
Now pay close attention cause my Father is about to
turn it around!
What was meant for our evil, God will turn around for
our good
This spiritual battle has become visible-to manifest God
like we should!

It's a collision between two kingdoms-darkness and
light
It depends on what kingdom you live in to have His
glory and His might!
God uses things He's not the author of so His glory can
be your quest
A good foundation is not proven until there's a storm-
that is your test!

Some trust in their money and other's in their might
But if we remember the name of the Lord-our battles
He will fight!
God's goodness is hidden within us all
Why is it only brought out when we have a great fall?
But our hidden God will show up-for He is our godly
tower

We must remember Him always and not just for this hour!
God will make His name remembered-in your heart this must sit
He is the God of this nation and all Americans must not forget it!

He chose this to be His nation a long time ago
That's why we are protected and blessed a whole lot more!
The people who said we couldn't pray will be underground
For when He wants His name remembered they can't be around!

The purpose of remembering is to return to the Lord
As soon as the troubles are over-you will forget about the poor!
It's not your blood, it's His blood-we must come to Him or perish
We are great because of God; it's His name you must cherish!

Don't think all the evil in the world is somewhere else
If we do we will not turn-let's look inside ourselves!
We have put money into everything, even things that we have doubt
A part of remembering Him is to bring His tithes into His storehouse!
Remembering Him is just one of the things that we have learned
His love for you will never change, but it is time you to turn!

A Perfect Father

One thing I need to make perfectly clear
God is a good God-and He hasn't given you the spirit
of fear!
Trials and tribulations will come in your life
You're going to need God to help you fight!
It's the devil's job to kill, steal, and destroy!
He will step on your life-as a little boy does a toy!
Don't blame my Father for the sins you have planted
Be obedient to His word and also His commandments!
Then when trouble comes you will know He is there
To comfort you in your trouble He really does care!
And things that happen that you don't understand
Just trust in Him-for He loves you like no one
else can!
I said trust in Him and have no doubt
I wouldn't serve a God you could figure out!
And He's not the author of anything bad!
Commune with Him and read His word-He's a perfect
Dad!
And if you love the Lord-no matter what you may go
through
He said He will never leave or forsake you!
He knows the future and the things you will need
He will use it to prepare you-out of your spirit you
must believe!

All Glory to God!
He is the End!

About the Author

A variety of poems inspired by my life
Before I knew the Lord and after I saw the light!
Some with emotions from me and my friends
Some are from a loss-most are from a win!
I found out the Lord was on my side
Now in the name of Jesus-it's the devil that has to hide!
For it's the blood of Jesus that protects me like nothing else can
My Father gave His Son and He was a perfect man!
Trials and tribulations try to take me from my praise
I will praise Him through the storms-His word is what I'll say!
For His word will last forever-eternity is a long time
Not only did He shed His blood for me, but for all mankind!
So come as you are, but you won't stay the same
Now that heaven is your destiny, my Father will change
you in Jesus name!

Author Contact Information

E-Mail: krlbpoetry@aol.com

To order a personal signed copy of KRLB go
to: www.myspace.com/krlbpoetry

Printed in the United States
45925LVS00002B/286-369

9 781932 503579